An Inherited Epic of Gilgamesh

Graeme Hetherington

An Inherited Epic of Gilgamesh

A poetic memoir dedicated to James McAuley

Many thanks are due to Ralph Spaulding for his more than twenty years of involvement in the development of this poem.

Acknowledgement is due to the following publications in which many of these poems first appeared:
The Age, *Antipodes*, *The Australian*, *The Canberra Times*, *Famous Reporter*, Fullers, Ginninderra Press, *The Mozzie*, *Poetry Matters*, *Poetry Monash*, *Prospect*, *Quadrant*, *Southerly*, *Studio*, *Valley Micropress* (NZ), *Westerly*.

An Inherited Epic of Gilgamesh: A poetic memoir dedicated to James McAuley
ISBN 978 1 76041 671 3
Copyright © text Graeme Hetherington 2019
Cover images by courtesy of John Elliott Classics Museum, University of Tasmania
Front cover: Neo-Assyrian cylinder seal, composition material, c. 850–600 BC (modern impression); the seal bears a scene of contest between two bird-like creatures, one apparently with a human head
Back cover: Mesopotamian clay tablet, 2052 BC; the tablet is a receipt recording, in cuneiform, the payment of two measures of barley as interest on a loan.

First published 2019 by
GINNINDERRA PRESS
PO Box 3461 Port Adelaide 5015
www.ginninderrapress.com.au

Contents

Prologue	7
The Literary Bonding of Gilgamesh and Enkidu	10
The Sexual Bonding of Gilgamesh and Enkidu	15
The Forest Journey	23
Gilgamesh and Inanna	31
The Death of Enkidu	34
Gilgamesh and the Death of Enkidu	36
Gilgamesh in Search of Immortality	40
Encounters With Hell's Gates' Monsters and Others	47
Intimations of Immortality and its Loss	55
The Return to Hobart Town and the Coming Death of Gilgamesh	61

Quotations introducing the eleven sections are from N.K. Sandar's translation of *The Epic of Gilgamesh*, Penguin Classics, 1972, and can be found as follows: section 1, p. 61; 2, p. 67; 3, p. 67; 4, p. 71; 5, p. 87; 6, p. 89; 7, p. 96; 8, p. l01; 9, p. 97; 10, p. 114; 11, p. 117.

Prologue

He was wise, he saw mysteries and knew secret things…

'The mad, bad, dangerous to know,
He'll use you up then spit you out'
From jealous folk, I'd counter with
The Karamazov clan in one,

Faust, Mann's holy sinner Grigorss
Who sloughed off shame beneath a rock,
Emerging honey-sweet and mild,
The Dioskouroi, star and shade

In interchanging roles, such was
The range his tightrope stretched across.
Enigmatic, I'd concede, doomed
To fall apart from paradox,

And yet he didn't, bearing all
Courageously within. Good friend
To me as was Uruk's god-king
To Enkidu delivered by

Royal courtesans from Hell's Gates' beasts
For civilising at his five
Year-long crab-shadowed final feast,
He was as poet, editor,

Musician, literary hoaxer, sage,
Both multi-talented and lone,
All said and done, Christ-crosser of
The great Australian emptiness.

Lapsed Protestant turned communist,
Then Catholic, pro-Vietnam war,
DLP, arch-conservative,
Administrator, ASIO

Grey Eminence, or spook, and all
In honour of life's ports of call,
Of 'Know Thyself' unfolding like
A blighted rose, he cut his cloth

Too large to fit his lesser foes
Who praise him better than I can,
Since any condemnation of
A struggle to be truly whole

Is eulogy indeed. To guard
His 'Music Late At Night' from those
Who'd turn it up loud tracing Trakl
Incest-and-death-by-drugs motifs

To actual ruthless hunts and kills
In private life for images,
Shrink sacred Art to human size,
He painstakingly crafted out

Anthropomorphic worms of 'who' –
The maggots of mortality
That rot as surely as the one
That fastened onto Enkidu –

To tracklessness, until he knew,
Repolishing, they'd no way back,
But curled, slipped from the surface of
His transcendental, deathless poems.

The Literary Bonding of Gilgamesh and Enkidu

Gilgamesh said, 'I shall befriend and counsel him.'

(i)

Scholastically unqualified,
A university 'ring-in',
Guilt drove me alcoholic from
Teaching the Classics second-hand,

Using translations others made,
Including the one I loved most,
The Gilgamesh epic. And while
On study leave in Baghdad, based

In various institutes' ill-lit
Archives and stacks researching it
Hallucinations overwhelmed,
Accumulated dust on books

Iraq's desert sands threatening to
Asphyxiate me for my crime,
The silverfish the monsters my
Hero confronts in Tablet nine,

Which I knew even then were mine
To fight if I could only find
The courage to resign and write
My own version in modern dress.

(ii)

A grey day at Conningham Beach,
You gave an off-the-cuff talk on
Aeneas to the Classics' Club,

Stressing his pietas and sense
Of duty to the future world.
Then staff and students walked with you,

Enthralled as you enlarged upon,
With detailed reference to key lines
Of *The Aeneid* known by heart,

The passion of Rome's founder for
His task, yours also evident,
Despite remarking that the tide

Was out and showed with plastic, tins,
What we'd come to, even in your
Qualified enthusiasm

Requesting a copy of my
Much annotated version of
The Gilgamesh epic à la

Heidel, to read at leisure, tired
And ill, my lectures on man's first
Poem wrestling with the fear of death.

(iii)

By party's dawn-grey end he felt
He'd groomed me well enough to trust
With his despair, confiding that

His 'solitary savage heart'
Had all but been burnt-out by life
As it had come his way to live,

And showed, for reading then and there,
Black-winged Irkalla at the door,
An epic's invocation to

Our muses, the shared red- and dark-
Haired hetaerae, beseeching them,
His 'twilight days' abyss of joy'

That now he joked 'closed at a touch',
To stay on when he'd gone, and in
The story's different female roles

Inspire me to finish the work
As Gilgamesh, the time come round
To swap our previous parts, with him

As Enkidu in his aspects
Of fallen mortally ill boon-
Companion terrified of death.

(iv)

My soul, almost extinguished by
The shadow of Van Diemen's Land,
Lit up when he bequeathed to me
The fledgling lines. In grief and joy

I labour to complete the gift,
Which proves how sharply he'd perceived,
That, invocation sown, I might
As epic lived write well enough,

Each poem a setting out and quest
For immortality, my quills
Plucked from the Hell's Gates' dragon's wings.
But there are days, when feeling un-

Worthy and ill-equipped I quail,
Have doubts, as my quatrains about
The ghost of Dante in the church
At Ravenna bear witness to:

To night I didn't rise in rage-
Red, soaking wet doctoral robes,
Perversely pretending it was
To vary the sacristan's dreams

And startle the wits out of monks
Asleep at their pre-dawn prayers,
When Jacopo, my poet-son,
But second-rate, had caused the sweat

To break out in my soul enraged
By his attempts to re-compose
My 'lost' thirteen cantos. Instead,
I passed as dry as a bone, clean

As a whistle through the tomb's lid,
My agony resolved at last.
And now, wrung out to truth, sun up,
I'm fit to give the blessing of

Good news, show where I hid them for
The boy to have a chance to share
In my posterity if he
Were equal to enhancing it.

The Sexual Bonding of Gilgamesh and Enkidu

Gilgamesh told his dreams and the harlot retold them to Enkidu.

(i)

Your eyes flashed 'Go to hell,' when I,
Adoring you in callow youth
And liking to think I was there
Already, identified with

You as a poet who might die
From an excess of loneliness.
I see now that I was half-mad
From infatuation with you,

And did this less to ease your Fate
Than mine projected as 'You need
Me for your soulmate, or you'll end
Up like poor Friedrich Hölderlin,

A schizophrenic alone with
Imaginary Diotima
And a piano for when words
Fall short of idealising her'.

Your look's imperative obeyed
And tolerance of self acquired,
I've grown to be more worthy of
Our one shared love, the perfect poem.

(ii)

Waiting for you I would look in the mirror,
Watching for you to come down the stairs
Into the bar, turning glass after glass
Of cognac around in my hands.

We would have one drink together
And leave, warming my hands in yours.
You have never come down those stairs,
And I am still looking into the mirror.

There are days when I want to live,
To smash the mirror and leave without you,
Learn how to love what is here.
You would come as I looked away,

The mirror in bits and pieces
Like treachery done to a dream.
But the mirror has claimed me forever,
And one day you'll come down the stairs,

Brushing the veils of cobwebs aside
With hands as white as snow.
I will turn from the mirror and see
Someone – someone the dead split image of me.

(iii)

My right to be the first with brides
Depends not just on being two-
Thirds god and king, but on how well

I read signs in red roses, blood-
Flushed symbols of male sexual pride.
Although no gardener, I alone

Attend their needs, admire, delouse,
Prune, water, wear, let none within
A bull's roar to ensure that I

Monopolise such power. They've bloomed
Less fully lately, and on dry
Thin brittle stems new thorny growth

Surrounds, choking to signify
The bridegrooms' rising. While this bud
In haughty isolation curled

Suggests a rival, a young man
Who's to be either nipped and thrown
Upon the compost heap, or dubbed

Soulmate and used to help out with
My exercising of *droit de
Seigneur* among more maidens than

I've appetite for now I'm doomed,
Cankered with cancer like the flowers.
Literally covering for me, he,

Rewarded with joy, can at least
Be then called on to bear his fair
Share of the husbands' mounting wrath.

(iv)

Presenting me with a red rose
She then joined me in bed, her flow
Of auburn hair a tent of fire
Enfolding us as we embraced,
Brightening and flaring, as she said
'I come as priestess, courtesan,
From Gilgamesh who's known me,
Empowered thus to give his gift
Of love. Received, it will free you
Trapped in the wilderness of need',
And afterwards I woke to sun
That seemed at first to be his face,
This poem my flower in return,
Forty years on since it was sown.

(v)

(For the Dark-haired Courtesan)

Creatures with a heavy rise and fall of breath,
Humped sheets of water move beneath the bridge.
Timed by a changeless law towards the beach
Rhythmically they build, each to their release.

We stand apart and watch. Legs could give way.
Our fingers lock. Your smile replenishes,
Makes good what I forget: close is only near
To him but all I have to try and grasp.

Double-backed we build, upwards like a wave.
Systole and diastole of our hearts can lull
Twin beasts of separateness: I listen to
Waves break, endlessly towards renewal.

(vi)

For favours done you paid for lunch
And then the evening barbecue
It grew into, starting the dance
Around the fire, during which I
And our two courtesans intoned

'You are the master!' and received
As our reward your devilish smile
Illuminated by the flames.
Tomorrow you were flying off
To Salzburg with the dark-haired one

As nurse, muse, lover in your search
For death poems à la Georg Trakl,
Since as her teacher, I'd agreed
To falsify attendance sheets,
Defer exams, all in the cause

Of Art's transcending laws you wished
To stay loyal to until the end,
And which I, besotted by you,
Overwhelmed as Pentheus was
By Bacchus, proudly sanctioned, as

I did your cynically cool romp
Into my hopeless marriage, which
Children had brought acceptance of,
Adored cruel god who broke me down
Into a love of poetry.

(vii)

It's always been a mystery,
The nature of my friendship with
This two decades older sick man.
I didn't love him physically,

Only the poet and his work,
The one role model that I've had,
Yet hungered for the women he
Apart from his wife seemed to have

In flocks. He tolerated it,
Even encouraging my need,
Setting up two *ménage à trois*
And playing such tricks after lunch,

But never sex together, as
Manipulating to ensure
That I, the drunkest of the three,
Drove the red-haired courtesan's car

For the first time, chauffeured them, all
Over each other in the back,
Leering and smirking at me in
The rear-vision mirror as far

As his home to drop just him off,
Leaving me with her for my turn
At closeness now she had his smell.
What was it meant to mean for him

Who on the other hand could tease
With talk of Aschenbach's late-life
Infatuation with a youth
In Thomas Mann's *Death In Venice*?

For me this sexual sharing that
Grafted not skin but soul and led
To my marriage already on
The slippery slope being destroyed

Was worth it for the poems it gave.
Was this his gift to me, to teach
That Art was the highest pursuit
And justified the sacrifice

Of others if they threatened it?
Since he, enraged, once said he was
No 'wishy-washy humanist',
When I, misunderstanding him

Had hung this round his neck. Or was
He, truth be known, all said and done,
His cancer terminal, depressed,
Spiritually bereft and lost,

Irresponsibly embarked on
A wild, traditional last fling,
Cynically bidding us farewell,
To give the other hetaera's

Dark but perhaps most accurate,
Entitled-to-theory, since she
As Irkalla, goddess of death,
Was closest to him at the end?

The Forest Journey

What man would willingly walk into that country and explore its depths? …weakness overpowers whoever goes near it: it is not an equal struggle when one fights with Humbaba…

(i)

Teeth bared from weight loss cancer caused,
You joked about it as we lunched
All afternoon, tête-à-tête in
Hobart's first licensed restaurant:

'Better a semicolon than
A full stop', then snarled 'piranhas!',
Envious of the appetites
Of fellow munchers chomping steaks,

Your fare champagne and ice cream as
You knocked with bony knees beneath
The table, skeletal hand clamped
Over both mine to further graft

Perpetuation of self through
My writing after you were dead.
Two decades younger and confused
About adoring you, I used

A mix of alcohol and pills
To stop palms sweating and to wipe
Out tension guilt and shame as you,
Snake-like with trembling bird at times,

Transfixed me with a gaze I read
As willing me to die instead,
At others as hunting me down,
Mocking, taunting, amused across

A party's crowded room, on stairs,
In toilet mirrors, bars, streets, lifts,
University corridors,
Stalking with steady looking till

I stood up tall in ownership
Of what in those barbaric, raw
Tasmanian 'blossom'-bashing days
I didn't have the strength to be:

A fledgling poet, who, to win
His wings must first, given his deep,
Childhood psychological wound,
The need to have his crushed soul re-

Cast in a sympathetic mould,
Serve an apprenticeship as shy,
Drug-propped, wild West Coast Enkidu
With kingly, two-thirds god, urbane,

Sophisticated Gilgamesh.
Your role held up for seven years,
Despair and cynicism swept
Aside or qualified with lines

You translated from Aeschylus:
'Cry sorrow, yet let good prevail,
Mankind must suffer to grow wise',
Or at your very best you'd chant

The Lord of Uruk's words, 'the dream
Was marvellous, the terror great,
It must be cherished at all cost'.
But then the big C took almost

Complete control in your last months,
Reducing your mind to 'we prey,
Are preyed upon' as you'd prove by
Leaning uncomfortably close,

'Are crucified and crucify'
You'd snap, as I, at sea about
How best to console, opted for
The part of Ganymede: a quick

Refill for Zeus, as tragically
You rolled your wistful eyes right back,
Like Oedipus, who'd put his out
Because life wasn't to be borne.

Your Torquemada mask back in
Place till the grape wore off again,
The worst cracks, widening, showed through to
'Everything's equally worthless,

The Pope knows God doesn't exist,
But that it's best to keep the myth,
Since people can't get by without
Comforting illusions. At heart,

Beneath the necessary lies,
I'm still, as in adolescence,
An atheist and anarchist'.
Chameleon-like, you'd intersperse

It all with a paternal, yet
Half-teasing, not quite neutral pat,
Suggesting sinisterly that
One more glass should anaesthetise

My booze-scarred pancreas for now
At least, then smirking at the Crown
Solicitor dining nearby
With low-browed pimply nance, imply

'But look what I've got on my hook!'
Almost six p.m., click achieved,
You'd load the boot with 'mother's milk',
Ham mincing walk, fond looks until

In harness off you'd drive, relieved
That *Götterdämmerung*, or 'clean-
Up time', as you would say, was nigh,
That your advanced cirrhosis was

Still less likely to kill you than
The carcinoma, socially
The more respectable disease.
Thus was by chance our last adieu,

My deeply flawed self in thrall yet
To you I'd enthroned, idolised
As good and evil, near-divine,
Who gave me life, though first you made

Me watch you flush a kitten down
The loo, which meant if ever I
Should kiss-and-tell you'd bring about
My premature demise as well.

(ii)

(Hofburg Palace Gardens, Vienna)

Sculptured Homeric scenes of war,
Grim double-headed eagles, lions,
Great-bollocked, rearing horses, kings
Astride to show who rules, provide
The monumental milieu for

A rally where the populist
Georg Haider harangues hordes with what
They want to hear, plans that will kill
Time hanging heavily on hands
Familiar with more active use.

It goose pimples skins leathery as
A crocodile's, tenses up slack
Old buttocks, while march music stirs,
Blurs eyes that run the flag's two strips
Of red into the one of white,

Provoking memories of '*Sieg Heil!*'
Nor am I, passing through by chance
As madness climaxed in the need
For police, proof against the blood's
Wild call threatening to sweep away,

A risk that led in this case to
A sublimation of the worst,
To you imagined by my side
With that other Georg, Trakl,
Admiring Paris hoisting high

'Blonde Helen', his 'opulent freight',
Images from a poem of yours
Translated freely from his work
That always managed to transcend
And transform evil into art.

(iii)

You said I'd be there at the end,
And so I am, if that meant in
Vienna in the autumn, late
In life and restless still as you

Were searching history-rotten streets
And suppurating parks for poems
That like those of Georg Trakl show
The soul-destroying decadence,

Despair and evil of the times.
Your works and his with me as friends,
I sit beneath Beethoven's bust
That with its 'Ode To Joy' visage

Would triumphantly dismiss them,
And honouring the truth the shit-
Brown leaves swarming my feet suggest
Defiantly read till it's dark.

(iv)

I've come to fancy that a snap
Of Trakl in a book of his
I'm mostly reading in an old-
World Viennese coffee house where
He might have sat mirrors my own

Anxious regard. Since after all
We have in common sister-love,
A mother cold as porcelain,
Drug addiction and poetry
That's therapy as well as art.

(v)

Avid of fame, we fought and slew,
With lines of poetry that scanned,
Humbaba, monstrous guardian of
The dark impenetrable woods

Of wilfully destructive post-
Modernism. The spawn of gods,
Unjustly they chose you alone,
As Enkidu, to die for this

Shared act of hubris. And then I
Dreamt of you, frantic with outrage,
Upturning boots which showed we'd failed,
That anarchy prevailed, lived on

As shit snaking about between
Hobnails, four rows of eight on each
Worn sole, that like our quatrains, made
Octosyllabically to beat

And pound in serried ranks, had stamped
In vain, the sightless heads of stools
Lifting to slither free and mock
Our hopes of chaos dead and gone.

Gilgamesh and Inanna

She said, 'My father, Gilgamesh has heaped insults on me, he has
told over all my abominable behaviour, my foul and hideous acts'

(i)

A fine-seeming pitcher that leaks,
An oven that lets in the cold,
Inanna, bitch-goddess of love
And war first tempts then destroys, leads

The stallion to tread in the pool
And muddy the water he drinks,
Embraces the lion with a net
Stretched over the pit she has dug,

And walks past my window in spring,
Swishing, ogling, luring until
I snap the blind down so I won't
Weaken and smile, give her the chance

To look away over my head,
Or cut it off with a sharp glance.
Revengefully she sent the Bull
Of Heaven to lay waste Uruk

With seven years of famine, drought,
And though Enkidu, as before,
Did no more than I in our feat
Of monster-slaying, save Shamash,

God of justice, the deities seized
On this to reinforce their will,
Again decree, that he, my life's
Only soulmate alone should die.

(ii)

Our 'deathless', 'indefinable',
'Ideal' love turned to touch and talk,
Instead of being pitched beyond
Their circumscribing, harmful reach

For soul to yearn intensely for,
As once it was when our eyes shone,
Enchanted by the morning star,
All things disintegrate and rot.

(iii)

An oleander flower fell
Onto the heart side of my shirt
Just as I wondered if you'd write.
It should have been the bitter leaf,

The curving green blade famous for
Its poison with the power to kill,
Since silence knifing rusts with age
And festers all I think and feel.

(iv)

I rang from overseas and saw
Our handset bedroom telephone
Unlifted from its cradle, pushed
Beyond your reach as laughingly
You made the beast with someone else.

Vibrating, on and on it shrilled
Despite my calling on the dot
Of our carefully prearranged time.
I hung up and it followed me,
But now as an implacably

Silent object in my mind's eye,
As still as stone and white as bone
With rigor-mortis grin from ear
To ear, till I imagined you
Lying as dead as it in bed.

(v)

When letters from your lawyers come
I philosophically agree
You need to break your promises
Too heartfelt to endure for long,

Dead calm and abstract understand,
World-wearily forgive, include
A short poem as the final word:
'Your marriage, health, art-teaching gone,

No children to divert bleak moods,
Of course our joint-owned house is yours
In which to wear your sadness well',
And condescendingly sign all.

The Death of Enkidu

…and he said to Gilgamesh, 'O my brother, so dear as you are to me, brother, yet they will take me from you.'

(i)

The sun had shone all summer long
Till life was just as sure as death,
Then autumn without warning signs
Was there one morning when I woke,

A greyness clamped on to the sky
As stunned with disbelief I rose
And felt the tiredness in my limbs,
My heart beneath my casual hand.

(ii)

The autumn sky is richly blue,
As deep and dark as what we know
Each dying year must bring about,
The sunlight distant, frail and chill

On leaves transparent with old age,
On children faintly touched with gold
Who blow white breath into the air
And watch it disappear like smoke.

(iii)

The window frame against the blind
Has made a cross as black as death,
A bird that hovers by my head
On long stiff wings that never flap,

And when I make it fly I learn
That out of sight's not out of mind
As darkness deep within green pines
Spreads slowly out to overwhelm.

(iv)

A landscape from Cezanne's last years
Once opened to my eyes and gave
An old man seated by himself,
Dear Death the friend he waited for,

An image that I've wondered at
Until today it came alive:
A blackbird singing here and there
Searched for me in an empty park.

(v)

A naked man-sized feathered thing
Sat waiting in a room for me.
It rose up darker than the night

On wings spread like Christ crucified.
I stabbed and stabbed and stabbed at it
As on and on it came at me,

Its smile more shocking than its wounds,
Until I knew I couldn't kill
My own death living on in me.

Gilgamesh and the Death of Enkidu

...seven days and seven nights he wept for Enkidu, until the worm fastened on him.

(i)

Limbs bent, foliage flat,
Drawn together as in pain,
Trees print themselves upon
A smudged blue winter sky.

Sleet-grey rolling clouds
Obliterate deep porticos
And palace hallways,
Shatter them to bits of blue,

Swallow up and bear away
Each impress of each tree.
But darkening storm winds drive
Pine quills sharp as nails

Until the sun must know and rise,
Be seen to climb and build
From the centre of the sky
A castle made of gold and blue.

(ii)

O Enkidu, you've become
A shadow lying in my arms,
A lyre of grief so tightly strung

I have no armament but song
To try and break the heart of Death.
O Enkidu, as we climb,

Blow breath softly through my hair,
Let your mirror be the moon,
Let me know you follow on.

O Enkidu, thin as air,
Give me still the faintest sign,
Let your shadow move near mine.

(iii)

Wreaths of red roses pressing on
The coffin lid, I fought off fear
Of breaking in and going too,
The thought that he was willing this,

And, paradoxical until
The end, that he was making me
Feel duty-bound to wed our shared
Dark-haired courtesan. And indeed

The choice was hard, since back home she
Lay in wait as Irkalla, or
As Ereshkigal, her two names
As goddess of the nether world,

Her bobby pins linked spider-like
And left lying around to scare.
I felt she'd badly let me down
As I struggled to change my role

From Enkidu to Gilgamesh,
Refusing to adapt and take
The parts I needed her in next,
That of barmaid Siduri, or

The kindly, sympathetic wife
Of immortal Utnapishtim.
I longed to find him, and to win
Eternal life now that I'd seen

The worm drop from my dead friend's nose
As he lay on his catafalque.
Revengefully, she wouldn't budge
From playing deity of death,

Since I, unlike her lord, the king,
Who at the end had cruelly dumped
Her foe, the other hetaera,
Our redhead, symbol of the sun,

For her exclusive kiss of death,
Had stayed light-blessed, partaking of
Her as an antidote throughout
My hero's grim, declining days.

Thus armed I didn't fear her dare,
The sinister suggestion that
I lie with her in his imprint
And either break their hold or die,

And rose triumphant, fleeing when
She claimed to dream of him below
Instructing her to wear her moist
Rank-smelling, steaming outfit of

Bird feathers every time we made
The beast where they had lain, until,
I understood, she'd smothered me,
Despatched to join him in death's realm

As consolation for his state,
Which, stripped of royalty, reduced
To ghostliness, to just one of
The disembodied, gibbering shades

Outnumbering the living, meant
Not only the same fate for me,
But serving him his food and drink
Of stagnant water, clay and dust.

(iv)

Again I have dreamt of you dead,
Leaf-thin on the softening ground,
Your skin drying out like a snake's
That fluttered as gently I kissed

Then woke without seeing you rise.
Today as I cut the long grass,
Uncovering things rotting and damp,
I choked on the taste of black earth.

Gilgamesh in Search of Immortality

Because of my brother I am afraid of death, because of my brother I stray through the wilderness and cannot rest.

(i)

(After a painting by David Keeling)

An empty, unsealed road means no
Impenetrably hard floor of
Darkness between myself and earth,

And bitumen to reinforce
Is out of place when shadows mat,
Stitch lace and coat to bind in strength.

As well, they isolate and change
Light into variously shaped,
Seemingly cool, transparent pools

I step into in summer on
My long hot walks now that I'm old.
But most invitingly of all,

It signifies the way ahead
Is unobstructed, and if by
A stroke of luck, the corner turned

It unfurls further, on and on,
Reprieve from my arrival once
More granted, then I'm filled with joy.

(ii)

(After a painting by David Keeling)

A corner of this life's road turned,
And there it is, I have arrived
At the last stretch of tunnel through
The typically dark woods that could

Entangle still from either side
Before I come out at the stair-
Way leading upwards to a key-
Hole filled with light of course, as in

The cliché that's not one when I'm
The person questing for this end
Of being able to unlock
The door and walk into the blaze.

(iii)

(Van Diemen's Land Road)

Strange moment on the road today
When I discovered that the stone
I'd nicely judged to kick along
Was tissue paper in a ball.
Instead of meeting, as it struck,

Resistance to its weight, my foot
Kept going, light as air, as though
At last I'd walked free of my un-
Loved self, discarded, flown off like
The wad of rubbish out of sight.

(iv)

Uphill on a loose gravel road,
The way to the forest seems far,
As hard as the one that grazed knees
In childhood if I fell with West

Coast Hell's Gates' bullies in pursuit.
But nearing the entrance that's like
A curtain separating day
From night, I suddenly, on this,

My seventieth birthday feel
Much lighter in body and thought,
And luxuriate as the weight
Of my life slips away, aware,

Flying along flat out to plunge
Into the soothing dark, that death
Will soon win in the race I've run
Since five to escape humankind.

(v)

It hurts to be always the guest,
The unwanted stranger who eats
And sleeps in another man's house.
He welcomes with water as much

To steady my nerves as quench thirst,
Refrains from enquiring at first
But finally asks for my name,
Birthplace, occupation and age

If he feels familiar enough.
The worst are the questions withheld,
The quick wondering looks as they shift
And offer a place in the group,

Make room at the table and share
The food barely covering plates.
Will he use his knife to cut meat
Or our tongues and eyes from our heads

For wagging and staring too long?
This evening from the dark yard,
Unable to join in I watched
The family happily talk,

Light flooding their faces with warmth
And panic my mind as I took
A tree in my arms and was home,
Night nailing me there with the stars.

(vi)

Tired after wandering for ten years,
Search fizzling out into vague 'God-
Alone-knows-whats', he fell for her
Rejuvenating red hair that

Proved grey beneath the dye, her fine-
Boned face glimpsed as his dead friend's, though
Potential for this soon was lost
In coarsening fat and folds. But he,

In need of creature comforts still
Threw in the towel and settled down
In Prague, Europe's diseased old heart,
With her, divorced mother of two

And cynically realistic Czech
Cardiologist who believed
Their history of invasion by
The Hapsburgs, Nazis, Communists

Had made them experts in the art
Of collaboration, how to
Survive regardless of the cost.
Deeply ashamed that he'd betrayed,

Corrupted by habitual ease,
The sacred quest summed up in man's
First epic as 'the dream was pure,
The terror great, and we must stay

Loyal seekers of it till we die',
The opposite of what she thought,
He nevertheless, paralysed,
Remained for two decades and cast

Her, eminently suited, in
The role of the divine barmaid
Siduri. Since she was an out-
And-out materialist evolved

From half a century beneath
The Russian yoke, and had pinned up
'Gather ye rosebuds while ye may'
In every room, all signed by Marx

And Engels, Stalin or Brezhnev,
Despite the English clergyman
Robert Herrick's authorship. 'What do
You mean?' she'd ask when he spoke of

The soul, answering him with 'such rot!'.
This and her halitosis from
Mouthing state slogans, and her drunk
Son shitting in the bath to show

His hatred of him, plus her crazed
Depressed dark daughter looking like
Irkalla, goddess of death, drove
Him from the fouled imperilled nest

To brave the lesser fears of dis-
Comfort and milder monsters on
The way to Utnapishtim, key
To gaining everlasting life.

Encounters With Hell's Gates' Monsters and Others

…and he fell upon them like an arrow from the string, and struck and destroyed and scattered them.

(i)

My father and my brother drawn
Together sharing skills of which
I was devoid, my mother cold,
Unbridgeably remote and lost
In her defeat, I had no one

To love until my sister came.
And then from fear of incest said
To occur in derelicts' shacks,
'No!' snapped at my release of joy
Drove me still further from the fold.

(ii)

A bird cries 'Innocent!', as though
It would acquit me, self arraigned
And judged guilty from childhood, when

Parents had caused me to lie face
To the wall in the bedroom shared
With my sister, afraid to sleep,

In case, to cut the knot of my
Growing confusion about her,
Guard down, I'd walk across and kill.

(iii)

My father's sexual arousal
When belting me, member outlined
Against his trousers swelling fit

To burst through, then confusing me
By kissing better with a smile
After mother had intervened,

And my nibbling at veg and fruit
To spoil his Harvest Festival
Display, his birthday cake just iced,

Cutting in half his golf balls to
Touch sticky white, made of us both
True Vandemonian grotesques.

(iv)

The woodshed housed our lavatory,
And round the back a small door low
Down in the wall gave access to
The dunny can. Emerging from
The long grass when my mother came,

Pregnant, to void her bowels, I'd turn
The latch and watch stools splash her bum,
Rending the veil of secrecy
My origins were shrouded in.
All went well till the thistles gone

To seed suggested that, instead
Of blowing them away to tell
The time, I tickle her. In rage
My father strode across the yard
And dragged me from the raspberry canes

That rattled as I shook with fright,
And with one tore a strip or two
Off my behind. That this was just
I have no doubt, and how could he
Delay expression of such wrath,

Not knowing that worse punishment
Awaited me in Athens, where,
Years hence, after a bender, I,
Hallucinating, fought off fear
Of turning into excrement.

(v)

(Mother Country)

A lowly Vandemonian
Alone in squalid English digs,
Half-crazed from drink and wrestling with
Personal problems and the past,

I've dreamt I'm Jack the Ripper, keen
To clean the strumpets up and win
The love of my cold mother, who,
Lusting after purity, wrapped

Childhood in a shroud. Their 'please guv,
Won't you keep a poor girl warm', taunts,
Until the red I see at such
A monstrous thought flows from their throats.

Then next I give a skilled display
Of surgery upon a corpse,
Excising rot in my bid still
To thaw her heart, fulfil her hopes

That I'll become a doctor, not
A long-haired, gender-confused bard.
But just before waking, scared stiff,
I see that every carved up pro's

Drained-looking, bluish, pink-tinged face
Is hers, as though I hate her too
And have displaced it on to them.
Enough blood left for her to blush,

Be it ever so faintly for
Her troubled, darling boy, I ease
Tension through gore-slimed fist into
The hulk-infested, filthy Thames.

(vi)

With pick and knife, I twice attacked
My brother, then I left him, leg
Gashed when the truck we rode derailed
Because I wouldn't use the brake
Despite his begging to get off.

As next he did the swing I pushed
And pushed from hatred of his bliss-
Fed face, that landed flat on blocked
Tear ducts the doctors' many probes
Failed even medically to fix,

Let alone problems of the heart,
My eyes now also watering, but
From age instead of the remorse
I think I ought to feel, yet can't,
When he was loved and I was not.

(vii)

I saw no beauty as a child
In any human soul or scene,
And later found myself to be

An ugly, cruel, misshapen thing,
The product of a world Des Finn
Could burst on like the shark in *Jaws*

Without the sinister grace of
The warning dorsal to redeem.
'Flake's' sentence served for setting cats

Alight with meths, my father bowed
To union reps' 'Fair go, he's paid
His debt, the cunt deserves a break,

You shouldn't stow the boots into
Even a mongrel if it's down',
And re-employed him underground.

Recovering from a jag when mine-
Horse Mary failed to budge a de-
Railed truck he beat her to slow death

With rusty line, and managed, then
And there, from wielding such a weight
To pass on first. But I can't let

Him go scot-free, and in my mind's
Eye he still lingers with DTs,
Where mares attaching to limbs drive

Him mad with fear of being torn
Apart, into the drink, with them
Astride, hooves pounding as he drowns.

(viii)

(University Colleague: for PRCW)

Dividing, conquering, you won
The Roman History Chair from where
You now survive destroying staff,
Intrigues to be vice-chancellor,

Wife's nervous breakdown, suicide,
And generally fulfil yourself
In dirty works that haven't found
A publisher. Dubbed 'Iron Man',

'King Rat', 'Unflappable', your dark
Suits still don't show wet hands wiped on
Them furtively, though sweat begins
To bead your upper lip from words

You use with less skill than before
Against colleagues' innuendoes.
Out walking Sunday with a new
Nit-picking departmental row

Instead of family picnicking,
These symptoms give me pause as I'm
About to kick a fissured stone
The shape and colour of a heart.

(ix)

(Studies in Brown)

Trembling, he loves easing into
Old-fashioned, Victorian-styled
Brown leather café chairs, to feel
Them yield until they're cavernous

Enough to snugly fit his booze-
Bloated disintegrating bulk
And give it a measure of peace,
Head well above the armrests, but

Still camouflage allowing him
To indulge comfortably in
A study named after their hue,
In the same range as excrement's

And those overwhelmingly sad
Paper bags waiters at the end
Of his day's intake always clothe
His naked need in to take home.

(x)

Desiring only peace, I sit,
A monster of sloth in the cool
Subaqueous shade of the park,
A latter-day Tiamat in

Her role of the annual spring flood
In Mesopotamia, or,
More correctly, its aftermath,
Stagnating with hate as I watch

My foe, the world's creator, god-
King Marduk as head gardener rush
Around, utilising me on
Loathed civilisation's behalf

And soaking summer-withered lawns.
But when, wanting something to do,
With violent assertion and noise,
He next becomes, provoked by my

Extreme passivity, a boy
With water pistol squirting till
My eyes are running like the twin
Rivers, Tigris and Euphrates,

I, stirred to the depths, overcome
Inertia and can't wait to rise,
To inundate again, and this
Time wipe life from the face of earth.

Intimations of Immortality and its Loss

As for you, Gilgamesh, who will assemble the gods for your sake, so that you may find that life for which you are searching?

(i)

(Fallen Angels)

Surely the Devil's very own
With thirteen Marsh Street its address
From early Van Diemen's Land times,
This loveless house built without soul
By surly chain-gang convicts in

Sweat-soaked sandstone from cliffs reduced
To ravaged faces, craters, pits
Reminiscent of Dante's Hell,
Was home to my dead hero, who,
As I revisited it late

One winter's evening seemed to be
The darkness that accompanied me
Into low-ceilinged, forlorn rooms
Where I imagined he, like me,
Poetically licensed, deceived

His wife with our two courtesans,
Inducing with pills, alcohol,
Sleep too deep for nightmares to wreck;
Then for fresh air, down garden paths,
Joined by memories of his rat-sized,

Neurotically yapping black pooch,
At ankle-height suited to nip
Achille's tendons till they snapped,
The Arch Fiend's creature dragging us
Past a wattle's rank rotting gold,

Beds of red roses cankered as
His flesh became, perhaps because
He wore in imitation of
Mephistopheles in Mann's *Faust*
A cheap loud-coloured check sports coat,

And lastly to dry lambless fields,
Rust-ruined pine trees pressing close
Beneath a moon- and star-lit sky
We wistfully regarded, but
Knew that we never would regain.

(ii)

The garden sleeps in green and grey,
Hydrangea heads in russet heaps
Like dead tea leaves upon the path,
But rose, camellia, jonquil flower,

Surprise me with their random song,
And round the corner as I climb
The rhododendron's outstretched arms
Are red with bursts of brilliant flame.

(iii)

Sky and sea and beach are bare,
As still and silent as a shell.
As ghost-faint as the daytime moon,

A cool breeze thins my heavy flesh
And husk of crab and feather weigh
Upon the lightness of my hand.

(iv)

The sand dunes welcome with their shapes,
The entrances like open arms,
A boneyard glinting where I find

White shells worn thin as wafered bread,
Time stripping me as wind strips rocks,
Salt water leaping clear like flame.

(v)

Light blue and hazy as a dream,
The hills seemed worn away, as though
A rending of the veil would show
Sky's nothing waiting to be sown

With hope, when suddenly, between
One heartbeat and the next, sand flew,
Stung skin and blinded, blanketing
And walling off the God we seek.

(vi)

Sand blown off the dunes like smoke,
The wind in fury built and wrecked
Sphinx, obelisk and pyramid,
The dead collapsing, hollowed out,

And as I sat selecting words,
Preserving what I thought and felt,
It whipped the pencil from my hand,
Huge storm waves curling in contempt.

(vii)

The wind has built high walls of sand
And carves out as it blows away
The frescos of an open tomb,
Where men and women come and go

In stories older than the hills,
The same as the Egyptians told:
Our only lasting human theme
The long procession of the dead.

(viii)

(Utnapishtim to Gilgamesh)

The ticket's condition is clear:
No turning back on the voyage
You didn't even choose to take,
And which, though short, is longest, since

It shadows and incorporates
All. Fearful, you can change wives, work,
Your house, country, jump real ships, go
Anywhere whenever you like

In actuality or dream,
Believe you are dodging your fate,
And still you're chained to time that needs
No relieving shift at the helm,

So constantly intent is it
On getting you there as programmed.
You can have one of heart – a change,
That is – becoming Death's best friend

By loving black in every form,
Hoping to be spared when at last
You sail into port, options gone,
As trapped as you were at the first.

(ix)

Insomnia striking as the long-
Haired unkempt bard at summer's height
Wanders through Greece endeavouring to

Write 'deathless' poems wishing they would
Renew hive-plagued scratched raw old skin,
He gives up wrestling for the words

And slips at last into deep sleep.
As did his hero, travel-stained,
World-weary, questing Gilgamesh,

Failing the test to stay awake
For seven days and nights to win
Eternal life. And then he plunged,

On his way home, bitter with loss,
Into the heaven of a pool,
Discarding on a sunny bank

Until he was refreshed, the next
Best thing to immortality,
His consolation prize called 'Plant

Of Youth', only to watch a snake
Coiled coldly but lovingly round
Its warmth glide off, newly cocooned.

(x)

(Charred Stump)

When death despatched my mentor-friend
I felt as any stump would do
That was left witnessing the tree
Go up in smoke that vanished too,

Its elevation to new heights,
Invisibly adding to non-
Existent God's cathedral of
Infinite nothingness, until,

Increasingly reduced by loss,
At life's end, forty years since his,
My own soul's desire equates with
His 'last hopeless wish not to be'.

The Return to Hobart Town and the Coming Death of Gilgamesh

He went on a long journey, was weary, worn out with labour, and returning engraved on a stone the whole story.

(i)

Finishing up, old and alone,
On European boulevards
Fruitlessly scanning verse on thumbs

And fingers, or just talking to
Myself, I felt, having left wives,
Job, country, parents, kids, to write

My epic poem, that, rightly so
It had abandoned me in turn,
When you, dead now for forty years,

Who'd inspired, set the task, appeared
In dreams strongly advising me
To do as in the prototype:

Return, and if I could withstand
What had first driven me away,
I'd wake one day able to soar

Again, and town elders then would,
As they did for Gilgamesh, have
Graffiti cleaned up, banned, and pass

Edicts allowing me to etch,
Tourists in mind, my tale upon
The university's bare walls.

(ii)

It's raining, as it's never rained,
Engulfing everything outside
And in, my eyes not filling just

From weakly muscled lower lids
In old age curling lashes back,
As after twenty years, returned

To convict- and near-genocide-
Based melancholy Hobart Town
I mourn at another's funeral

A long-dead friend and my life spent
Revengefully, unable to
Forgive the world, my family for

That grim inheritance, my Hell's
Gates' origins he tried to help
Me come to terms with, sublimate,

By setting me upon the road
To poetry. All done, a gaunt
Dark-haired girl reminiscent of

The courtesan escaped from, black
Umbrella spread Empire-wide, smiles
Like Death and asks me underneath.

(iii)

The fountain leaping peaks and falls
On stone, like wildly surging love
That has its moment of climax

Then hits rock-bottom, spraying up
Into an empty, glittering cage,
A smile that masks the hollowness.

(iv)

On a grey day, the first of March
To be exact, limbs heavy, tired,
I felt life ebb and drain away
As I looked at the water, still,

Too easily crossed, heard crows caw in
A gum whose red flowers dulled the more
I searched to make the black shapes out,
Guiltily waiting for the hours

To pass, for the evening news, when
It would be officially announced
That autumn had arrived, and thus
It was all right to feel this way.

(v)

(Fitzroy Park)

Among the tall, well-spaced dark pines
Encircling me, the autumn day
Is perfect, sunny, quiet and still,
Till in a trance, seeming to be

Without heartbeat or pulse, I lap
It up, luxuriating as
Time stopping like an old friend sits
Beside me on my usual bench,

When suddenly a sprinkler jets
Around, a silvery hand that turns
The park into a giant clock face,
Furiously whirling me on.

www.ingramcontent.com/pod-product-compliance
Lightning Source LLC
Chambersburg PA
CBHW062159100526
44589CB00014B/1878